Rustic Wedding FAVORS

For guest favors that reflect the theme of a rustic wedding, keep it simple with these DIY projects. They use burlap, kraft paper, peat pots, jute, and other natural materials to create elegant presentations of delicious treats, pretty plants, and fun items – including flip-flops for more comfort at the reception!

LEISURE ARTS, INC. • Maumelle, Arkansas

Birdseed Hearts

SHOPPING LIST

For 4 birdseed hearts:

- ☐ $^{3}/_{4}$ cup birdseed blend
- ☐ .25 oz. (7g) packet of unflavored gelatin
- ☐ heart-shaped baking pan or mold that will yield hearts about $2^{1}/_{2}$" wide (we used a silicone mini treat mold)
- ☐ $^{1}/_{4}$" diameter dowel
- ☐ 52" length of jute twine
- ☐ 4 kraft paper tags
- ☐ intertwined hearts stamp
- ☐ number stamps
- ☐ black permanent ink pad
- ☐ black fine-point permanent pen

To make 4 Birdseed Hearts:

Note: *Make the Birdseed Hearts as close to the wedding date as possible to preserve freshness.*

1. Stamp each tag with the heart stamp and the wedding date. Use the pen to fill in the couple's names. Cut the twine into four 13" lengths. Thread a twine length through each tag.
2. In a large mixing bowl, mix $^{1}/_{4}$ cup slightly boiling water with the gelatin, stirring until dissolved. Let cool slightly. Add the birdseed, stirring well to coat the birdseed with the gelatin mixture. If there is still liquid in the bowl bottom, add a bit more birdseed.
3. Firmly press the mixture into the baking pan or mold cavities, making 4 hearts. Press the dowel into the mixture near the heart tops to make holes for the jute hangers. Let the mixture set up overnight. Remove the hearts from the pan or mold and place on a paper towel to remove any excess moisture.
4. When the birdseed hearts are dry, thread the jute hanger through the hole and knot the ends together.

John
Carly
8 · 8 · 15

Burlap Bags

SHOPPING LIST

For each burlap bag:

- ☐ 6" x 12" piece of lace-covered burlap ribbon
  OR
  6" x 12" piece *each* of burlap ribbon & glitter dot tulle
- ☐ cork sheet (found in the scrapbooking department)
- ☐ letter stamps
- ☐ brown permanent ink pad
- ☐ jute twine
- ☐ heart-shaped punch about 2" wide
- ☐ 1/4" diameter hole punch
- ☐ sewing machine
- ☐ contents for bag

To make each Burlap Bag:

1. If making the burlap and tulle bag, layer the tulle on the burlap and treat them as one piece. For either bag, match the right sides and short ends and fold the burlap in half. Use a 1/2" seam allowance to sew the side seams ***(Fig. 1)***. Turn the bag right side out.

Fig. 1

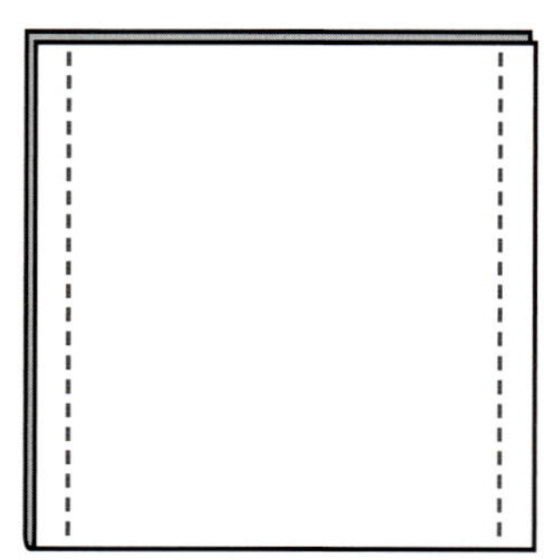

2. Carefully punch a heart from the cork sheet. Punch a hole near the top. Stamp the couple's initials on the heart.
3. Fill the bag. Thread the heart on a 15" twine length and tie the bag closed. Knot and trim the twine ends as desired.

K&P
K&P
K&P

Candied Apples

SHOPPING LIST

For each apple:

- ☐ candied apple (see recipe right or buy pre-made)
- ☐ well-washed, non-poisonous tree or bush stick
- ☐ green patterned cardstock
- ☐ decorative-edge scissors
- ☐ message stamp
- ☐ black permanent ink pad
- ☐ jute twine
- ☐ $^{1}/_{4}$" diameter hole punch
- ☐ tracing paper

To make each Apple:

1. Trace the leaf pattern onto tracing paper; cut out. Use the pattern to cut a cardstock leaf with the decorative-edge scissors. Stamp the message on the leaf and punch a hole at the base.
2. If using pre-made candied apples, replace the stick **OR** make the Candied Apples. Loop the jute through the hole in the leaf tag and tie the tag to the stick.

Candied Apples

6-8 apples, washed, dried & stems removed
6-8 well-washed, non-poisonous tree or bush sticks
2 cups granulated sugar
1 cup water
$^{2}/_{3}$ cup light corn syrup
$^{1}/_{2}$ to 1 teaspoon red candy coloring (not food coloring)
candy thermometer

Cover a baking sheet with wax paper; set aside. Press a stick into each apple; set aside.

In a large heavy saucepan, combine sugar, water, and corn syrup; place the candy thermometer on pan (do not let it touch the pan bottom). Without stirring, cook over medium-high heat to hard crack stage (300-310 degrees on candy thermometer). Remove from heat and stir in coloring.

Dip each apple in mixture and coat well. Let excess drain off and place on wax paper-lined baking sheet to cool. Makes 6-8 apples.

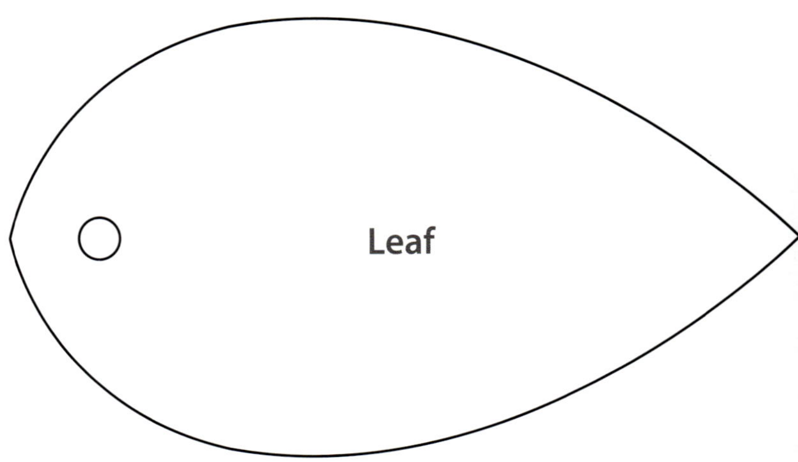

all you need is love!

Photo/Music CD Holder

SHOPPING LIST

For each cd holder:

- ☐ 12" x 12" sheet of brown cardstock
- ☐ 2" x 11" strip of newspaper
- ☐ 1 yard thin black cord
- ☐ 1$\frac{1}{2}$" wide unfinished wood circle tag
- ☐ letter stamp that will fit on tag
- ☐ message stamp that will fit on holder front (ours is 3$\frac{5}{8}$" wide)
- ☐ black permanent ink pad
- ☐ black permanent marker
- ☐ double-sided tape

To make each Holder:

1. Color the edges of the wood tag with the marker; allow to dry. Stamp the letter on the tag.
2. Place the newspaper strip on scrap paper. Lightly drag the black ink pad over the newspaper surface creating a smudged look.
3. Referring to **Fig. 1**, draw the shape of the holder on the cardstock and cut out.

Fig. 1

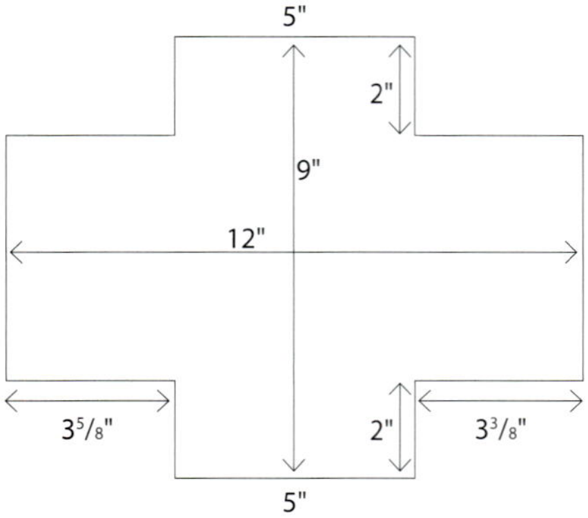

4. Center the CD on the holder and fold the flaps over the CD, starting with the top and bottom flap and ending with the wider 3$\frac{5}{8}$" flap.
5. Wrap the newspaper strip around the holder, overlapping and taping the ends with double-sided tape. Wrap the cord around the holder 3 times and knot, slipping the tag onto the cord before tying the final knot. Trim the cord ends as desired. Stamp the message on the holder front.

Happily ever after
M

Hugs & Kisses Nut Pots

SHOPPING LIST

For each nut pot:

- ☐ 3¹/₈" diameter peat pot
- ☐ 1⁷/₈" wide x 1" high unfinished wood oval
- ☐ "x" & "o" alphabet stamps that will fit on oval
- ☐ black permanent ink pad
- ☐ brown permanent wide marker
- ☐ natural-colored raffia
- ☐ tan tissue paper
- ☐ desired nuts (we used peanuts in the shell)
- ☐ hot glue gun & glue sticks

To make each Nut Pot:

1. Color the edges of the wood oval with the marker. Stamp "xoxo" on the oval.
2. Cut two 13" lengths of raffia. Thread the oval onto the raffia. Tie the raffia around the peat pot. Apply a bit of glue if necessary to hold the tag in place.
3. Cut a 10" square of tissue paper. Place the tissue paper in the peat pot and fill with nuts.

Cookie Bags

SHOPPING LIST

For each cookie bag:

- ☐ brown paper bag to hold cookie (ours are 4" x 6")
- ☐ colored paper doily (ours are $3^3/_4$" diameter)
- ☐ small tag (ours are $1^1/_8$" wide x $1^3/_4$" high)
- ☐ letter stamps to fit tag
- ☐ brown permanent ink pad
- ☐ light-colored jute twine
- ☐ cookies wrapped in plastic wrap

To make the Cookie Bag:

1. Stamp "LOVE" on the tag.
2. Place the wrapped cookies in the bag and fold the top over about 1". Fold the doily in half and place over the bag top. Wrap the twine around the bag and tie a bow. Tie the tag to one of the twine tails. Trim any excess twine.

Fire Starters

SHOPPING LIST

- ☐ dry pine cones (choose cones that are about 4" high & 3" across)
- ☐ candle-making wax (we used pink)
- ☐ waxed wicks & wick tabs
- ☐ paper sacks (ours are 4 3/4" wide, 3 lb paper sacks found in the party supply department)
- ☐ solid-colored cardstock
- ☐ patterned scrapbook paper
- ☐ double-sided tape
- ☐ decorative-edge scissors
- ☐ 1/8" diameter hole punch
- ☐ very thin jute twine
- ☐ clean, large tin can for melting wax
- ☐ electric skillet or sauce pan that can will fit in
- ☐ tongs
- ☐ cake cooling rack & newspapers

To make the Fire Starters:

1. ***Caution: Do not melt wax over an open flame or directly on burner.*** Cover work area with newspapers. Create a double boiler by placing the large tin can into the electric skillet or sauce pan. Fill the skillet or pan with a few inches of water. Place the wax in the can and allow it to melt over low heat.
2. While the wax is melting, wrap a candle wick around each pine cone, leaving a few inches of wick near the top of the cone.
3. Once the wax is melted, use tongs to dip a pine cone into the wax. Cover the entire pine cone with wax. Remove the pine cone from the wax and place it on the cooling rack to harden. Dip the pine cone in the wax again if desired.
4. For each fire starter, trim the paper sack to 3" tall when opened. Print the label and tag on patterned scrapbook paper and cut out with decorative-edge scissors. Adhere the label and the tag to cardstock with double-sided tape and cut out, leaving a cardstock border. Adhere the label to the sack with double-sided tape. Punch a hole near the tag top, loop a length of twine through the tag, and tie the tag on the pine cone. Place the pine cone in the sack.

Stacy and
Michael
Thank you
You Warm Our Hearts
Pine cone fire starters

"Kick Off Your Heels" Basket

SHOPPING LIST

- ☐ basket to hold flip-flops (our basket is about 12" wide x 9" deep x 5" high)
- ☐ flip-flops in assorted sizes
- ☐ unfinished wood piece for sign
- ☐ kraft paper tags (one for each pair of flip-flops)
- ☐ alphabet stamps (we used 3 different styles)
- ☐ brown permanent ink pad
- ☐ jute twine
- ☐ bakers twine
- ☐ chalk marker in desired color
- ☐ ribbon for basket bow (we used 45" of 1" wide ribbon)
- ☐ oval stencil or template to fit tag
- ☐ 1/8" diameter hole punch
- ☐ drill with 3/16" bit

To make the Basket:

1. For the basket sign, drill a hole in each upper corner of the wood piece. Use the alphabet stamps to stamp the message on the sign. Add colorful accents to the sign with the chalk marker. Attach the sign to the basket with jute twine, knotting the twine ends.
2. Tie a double bow on the basket side with the ribbon.
3. For each flip-flop tag, use the oval stencil or template to lightly draw an oval with a pencil on each tag. Add chalk marker dots in the oval shape. Once the chalk has dried, erase any visible pencil lines. Stamp the size of the flip-flops in the oval center. Punch a hole near the tag top and use bakers twine to tie the tag to the flip-flop pair.

S
M
L
KICK off your HEELS!
and stay a while
davis + merritt

Mint Rolls

Pick up some chalk markers to personalize a chalkboard tag! Tie the tag around a chalkboard serving plate.

SHOPPING LIST

For each mint roll:

- ☐ .75 oz. rolled package of mints
- ☐ corrugated paper
- ☐ patterned cardstock
- ☐ letter stamp
- ☐ black permanent ink pad
- ☐ thin natural-colored twine
- ☐ heart-shaped paper punch (ours is about $1\frac{3}{8}$" wide)
- ☐ $\frac{1}{16}$" diamete hole punch
- ☐ double-sided tape

To make each Mint Roll:

1. Cut a piece of corrugated paper that will fit around the mint roll (we cut our paper $2\frac{1}{2}$" x $2\frac{5}{8}$").
2. Place a piece of double-sided tape along one side of the mint roll. Wrap the corrugated paper around the mint roll, adhering the ends to the tape on the roll.
3. Stamp the letter on the cardstock. Centering the letter, punch out a heart shape. Punch a hole near the top of the heart.
4. Tie the heart on the mint roll with a 7" length of twine.

Peat Pot Candy Holder

SHOPPING LIST

For each candy holder:

- ☐ small peat pot, about 2 1/2" square at top & 2 1/2" tall; these may come as a multi-pot unit, but can be cut apart
- ☐ 1 1/2" wide unfinished wood heart
- ☐ message stamp that will fit on heart
- ☐ black permanent ink pad
- ☐ acrylic paint in desired color & small paintbrush
- ☐ thin jute cords in natural & desired color
- ☐ clear treat bag
- ☐ desired candy
- ☐ hot glue gun & glue sticks

To make each Candy Holder:

1. Cut peat pots apart if part of a multi-pot unit.
2. Cut a 36" length of both jute colors. Holding the lengths together as one and starting at the center of one side, wrap the jute around the peat pot 3 times. Knot the ends together. Tie a knot at the end of each tail and trim the ends as desired.
3. Paint the edges of the wood heart; allow to dry. Stamp the message on the heart. Glue the heart to the pot.
4. Cut a 6" length of both jute colors. Trim the treat bag to 5 1/2" tall. Fill with candy and tie closed with jute.

Potted Plants & Stand

SHOPPING LIST

- ☐ Large & Medium Basswood Country Rounds®
- ☐ 4" diameter x 3" high birch branch piece
- ☐ 2" diameter x 1/2" high birch branch piece
- ☐ dark grey cardstock
- ☐ white pencil
- ☐ white cotton string
- ☐ very small clay pots (one for each succulent)
- ☐ succulent plants and potting soil
- ☐ tracing paper
- ☐ 8 1/2" length of 3/16" diameter dowel
- ☐ 1/4" diameter hole punch
- ☐ hand drill and 3/16" drill bit
- ☐ wood glue
- ☐ hot glue gun & glue sticks

To make the Plant Stand:

1. Pot the succulent plants in the pots. Tie cotton string around each pot, trimming the ends as desired. Apply a bit of hot glue to the back of each pot to hold the string in place.
2. Use the wood glue to glue the large birch piece to the center of the large wood round. Center and glue the medium wood round to the large birch piece. Drill a hole in the center of the small birch piece. Glue the dowel in the hole. Glue the small birch piece to the center of the medium bass round.
3. Trace the flag pattern (page 24) onto tracing paper; cut out. Use the pattern to cut a cardstock flag. Punch holes as indicated on the pattern. Use the white pencil to write "thanks" on the flag. Slip the flag onto the dowel. Place the potted succulents on the wood rounds.

To make these favors even easier, check your local garden center or nursery for pre-potted succulents or other small plants!

Popcorn Crate

SHOPPING LIST

- ☐ unfinished wood crate (ours is 5³/₄" x 15" x 5")
- ☐ paper sacks to fit in crate (ours are 4³/₄" wide, 3 lb paper sacks found in the party supply department)
- ☐ large decorative-edge scissors
- ☐ chalkboard paper
- ☐ assorted washi tape with black background
- ☐ white chalk marker
- ☐ double-sided tape
- ☐ Design Master® Glossy Wood Tone Spray
- ☐ popcorn

To make the Popcorn Crate:

1. Follow the Wood Tone spray manufacturer's instructions to stain the crate; allow to dry.
2. Cut a piece of chalkboard paper to fit each end of the crate. Use the chalk marker to write your message and to decorate the paper. Adhere the papers to the crate with double-sided tape.
3. Trim the top edge of each paper sack with the decorative-edge scissors. Adhere a 4" washi tape length to each bag and use the chalk marker to write a message on the tape. Fill each sack with popcorn.

Love
is sharing your
Popcorn!

Seed Packets

SHOPPING LIST

For each seed packet:

- ☐ 8" square of brown cardstock
- ☐ desired packet of seeds
- ☐ 13" of 1" wide burlap ribbon
- ☐ floral stamp that will fit in a 3"wide x 4 1/2" high area
- ☐ brown ink pad
- ☐ 7mm light green gemstone
- ☐ craft glue
- ☐ craft knife
- ☐ tracing paper

To make each Seed Packet:

1. Trace the pattern (page 24) onto tracing paper; cut out. Use the pattern to cut the packet from cardstock. Use the craft knife to cut the slit as indicated on the pattern.
2. Stamp the floral image on the front of the cardstock. Glue the gemstone to a flower.
3. Fold and crease the cardstock as indicated on the pattern. Insert the packet of seeds in the cardstock packet; fold the packet and insert the tab into the slit to secure.
4. Tie the burlap ribbon around the packet.

Production Team: Product Development Director – Anna L. Andrews; Designer – Kelly Reider; Contributing Designers – Kim Hamblin and Becky Werle; Technical Writer – Mary Sullivan Hutcheson; Technical Associate – Frances Huddleston; Editorial Writer – Susan Frantz Wiles; Senior Graphic Artist – Lora Puls; Graphic Artist – Cailen Cochran; Photostylist – Lori Wenger; Photographer – Jason Masters.

Patterns

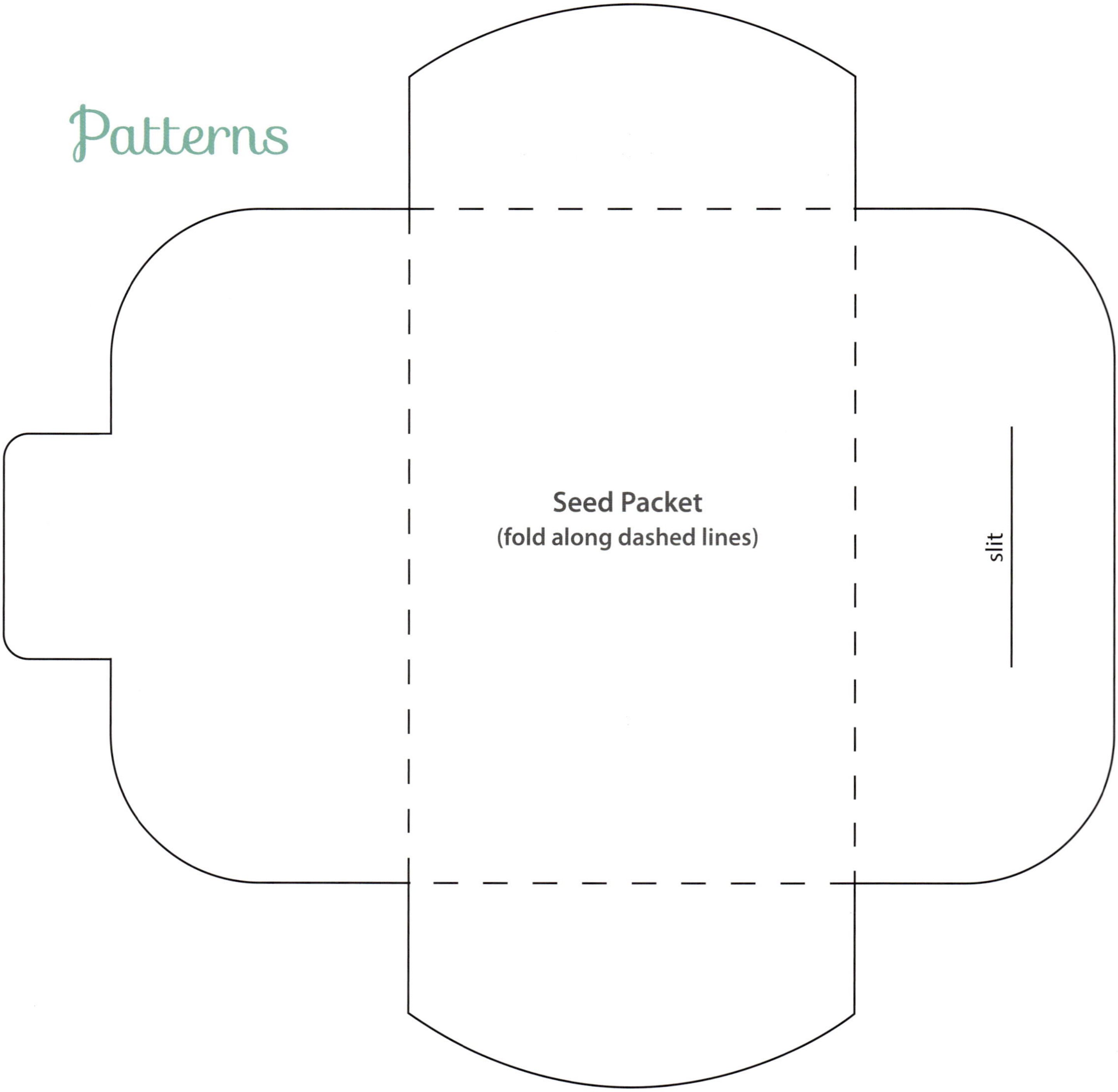

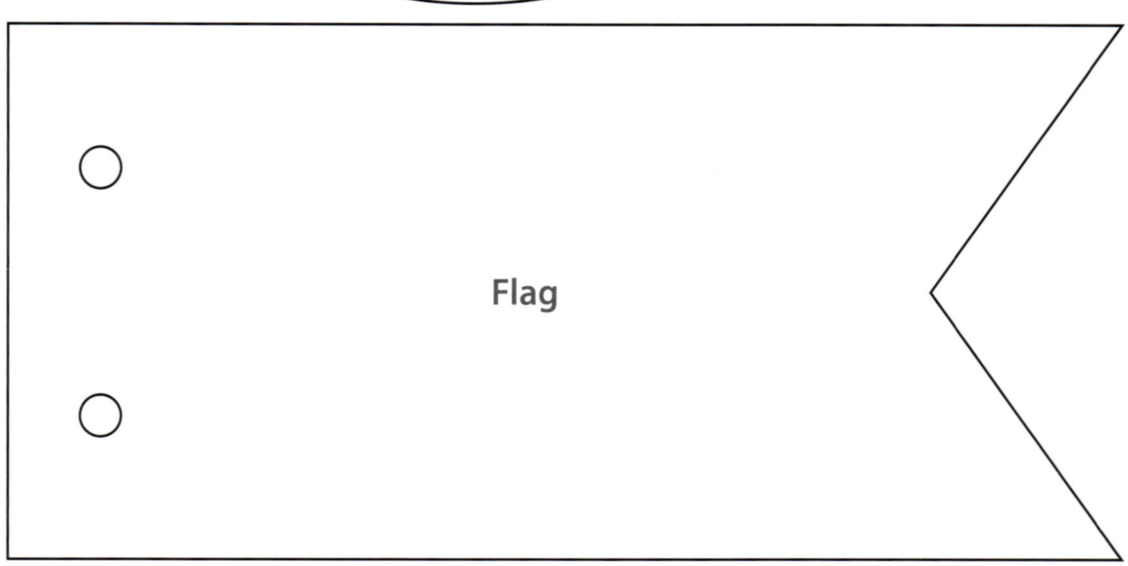